HI-TECH JOBS WITHOUT COLLEGE

BE A DATA CENTER TECHNICIAN

by Sue Bradford Edwards

BrightPoint Press

San Diego, CA

an imprint of ReferencePoint Press, Inc.
Printed in the United States

For more information, contact:
BrightPoint Press
PO Box 27779
San Diego, CA 92198
www.BrightPointPress.com

LIBRARY OF CONGRESS CATALOGING-IN-PUBLICATION DATA

Name: Edwards, Sue Bradford, author.
Title: Be a data center technician / by Sue Bradford Edwards.
Description: San Diego, CA: ReferencePoint Press, 2026 | Series: Hi-tech jobs without college | Includes bibliographical references and index. | Audience: Grades 7–9
Identifiers: ISBN 9781678212643 (hardcover) | ISBN 9781678212650 (eBook)
The complete Library of Congress record is available at www.loc.gov.

CONTENTS

AT A GLANCE

- A data center is a building or room full of computers called servers. These centers store and provide the data smart devices use each day.
- Data center technicians maintain a network of servers. They repair, update, and expand the hardware as needed.
- People rely on data center technicians to keep data flowing.
- Some people go to college to train for this job, but a degree isn't required.
- Certifications provide a pathway to a career as a data center technician.
- Internships offer people the chance to get hands-on experience as data center technicians.

- Data center technicians often work in teams.
- With experience and training, a data center technician can earn a promotion. The person might become a team leader or a maintenance manager.
- More data centers are built every year. This means data center technicians will continue to be needed in the future.

A DATA CENTER TECHNICIAN'S DAY

Every day, people go online. They take online classes. They use social media. They stream movies from services such as Disney+. Data center technicians, or DTs, make all this possible. They work in data centers.

A data center is where computer systems are stored. It can be one room in a business. Or it can be an entire building.

Data center technicians check to make sure files are being backed up each day.

Data centers are designed to house servers. Small data centers have 500 to 2,000 servers, while the biggest ones have 5,000 or more.

PARTS OF A DATA CENTER

Data centers have many parts. These physical parts are called hardware. Hardware includes servers and storage systems. Servers are powerful computers. They run programs and store data. Many servers are connected to form a network. This is a system of connected devices. The network allows machines to communicate with one another. It allows information to be shared between these machines and outside users.

Other hardware is part of the network, too. Routers direct data through the network. Switches connect servers. Cables connect these parts together. Firewalls protect the network. They block people who aren't allowed to access the network.

Brittany Gates is a DT. She works at a Google data center. She keeps the hardware updated. This prevents failures. Gates installs new switches and routers. When a **vendor** installs new cables, Gates makes sure they work.

If the cables don't work, she must find out why. She checks to make sure they are plugged in correctly. Then she checks switches. She looks to see if the switches were installed properly. Then she confirms that the switches work. Gates is one of the DTs who makes sure the parts in the network work together.

WHAT DOES A DT DO?

A DT maintains the computer network. They may have other responsibilities, too. At Google, they help install networks in new data centers. They also maintain the connection to the electrical grid. Computers create heat. DTs at Google's data centers maintain the systems that keep them cool.

DTs know the data center and its **infrastructure**. These systems make the data center work. They provide power. They keep the servers cool enough to run.

DTs run the cables that connect servers and other hardware. They also make sure the cables are plugged in correctly.

DTs work at companies such as Amazon and Google. Banks, hospitals, and government departments also hire DTs. In March 2025, there were more than 5,400 data centers in the United States. The number of data centers will grow as online services become more important.

CHAPTER ONE

EXPLORING DATA CENTER TECHNOLOGY

People often drive by data centers. But they might not know it. The buildings are often large. Some look like warehouses. They don't have windows. They are built only to house servers. These data centers may include only the basics for workers. Others look more like office buildings. They may have lobbies and meeting rooms.

"Data centers are specially designed structures that are created to hold

In early 2024, there were more than 11,800 data centers around the world.

DTs check servers and other equipment at a data center multiple times each day.

thousands of machines," said Geoffrey Challen.[1] Challen teaches at the University of Illinois Urbana-Champaign. He explains that data centers are full of racks. These racks hold thousands of servers. Server computers don't have monitors. Technicians use their laptops to log into the servers.

The servers run all day, every day. This ensures that people can always use digital services. People use their phones, laptops, and smart watches to access these services. DTs make sure content is available online.

THE WORK OF A DT

DTs do many tasks. DTs may install hardware. This could mean bringing in new

The Cloud

When data is stored on servers connected to the internet, it is said to be in the cloud. These servers are located in data centers. They are accessed through the internet. Amazon and Google own cloud data centers. So do IBM and Microsoft. Companies pay them to use these cloud data centers. This is a good choice for a smaller company. The smaller company does not need to maintain its own servers.

Technicians use diagnostic software to help them locate problems in the network.

racks or adding servers. New servers need to be set up, or configured. A DT might install software such as Windows Server

Configuration Manager. This software allows other servers in the network to see the new server. It also helps the server do its job. That might mean storing data. Or it could mean providing search **optimization**. Servers may be set up differently for various uses. Without the software, the new server cannot do its job. This means it cannot gather the data that people need.

Sometimes, the flow of data across a network slows down. Other times, there is packet loss. This is when data is lost as it flows through the network. DTs **troubleshoot** these and other problems. They use **diagnostic** tools to find out what went wrong.

Some problems involve data transmission. Data is transmitted as light

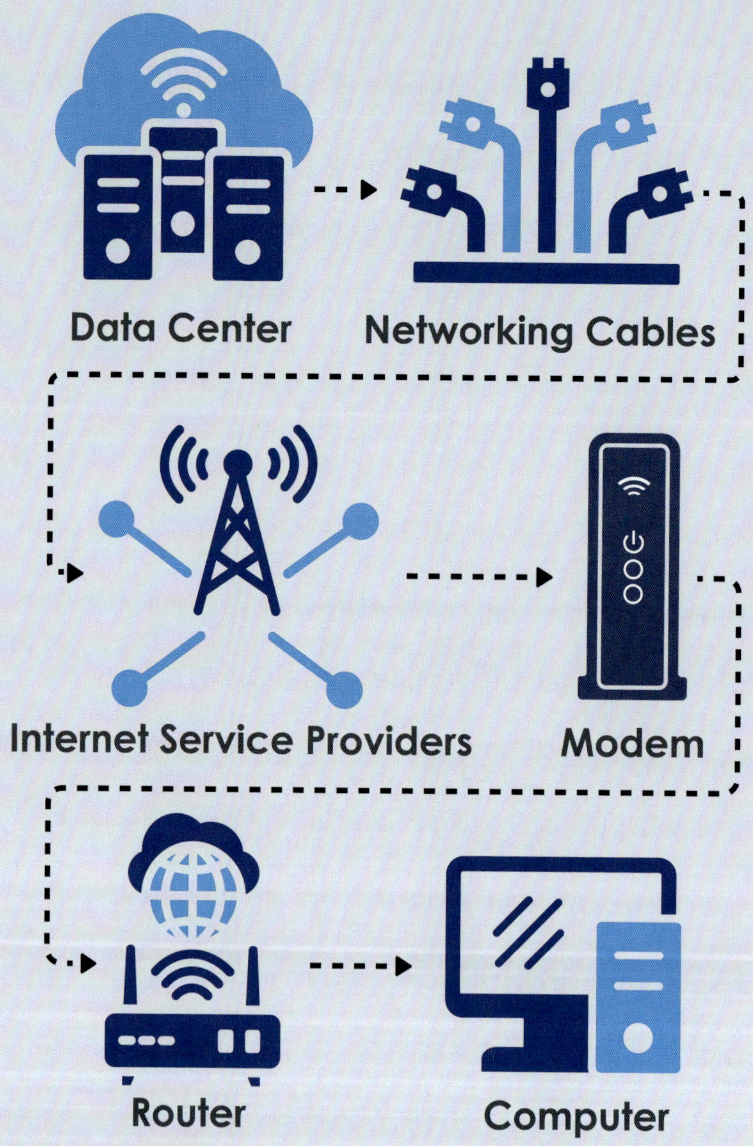

When a user types a question into a browser, the information moves from the data center to the user's computer through a specific path.

along fiber optic cables. DTs use fiber inspection scopes. These handheld tools have cameras. This allows DTs to examine the fibers. They look for dirt. Dirt blocks the flow of light. DTs also use network testers. These tools check how fast data is being sent. Network testers also check error rates. They note the number of errors, too. With the right tools, the technician can find the problem.

Some DTs also make repairs. Adrian McClanahan worked as a DT. She described the skills needed to make repairs. "You need to have a good understanding of and be comfortable with touching the computer parts," she said.[2] McClanahan explained that this can be as basic as running a new cable.

OTHER ABILITIES

DTs need to learn **inventory** management as well. This means knowing which parts they have. When they use a part, they must note this. They also track when it is time to order new parts. This helps ensure they have the parts they need for repairs.

Sometimes DTs handle data security. Data security means blocking **unauthorized** access to computer systems. This might mean blocking an unauthorized user who tries to log on. It could mean blocking malware. Malware is harmful software such as a computer virus. It could be spyware that gathers information.

To add security, DTs do more than set up firewalls. They also review access logs.

Logs are computerized lists. They keep track of who requests data. The log lists when the request was made. It lists the data that was accessed or saved. A log can help spot someone who should not have access

Networks that are protected by firewalls and passcode entry keep data more secure.

to a network. Sometimes, technicians work with security teams. Large companies such as Google have security technicians. They focus on securing data. Having these teams work together requires good communication.

COMMUNICATION AND OTHER SKILLS

There are other skills that DTs need. These include communication skills. DTs must be able to share information. They need to communicate clearly and effectively.

DTs have to be able to communicate face-to-face. They must share information with the people on their team. When something isn't working right, they must ask questions about problems people

DTs spend many hours on their feet and are required to move and install equipment.

had with the system. They need to be able to clearly describe to other team members what they have observed.

DTs also need to be strong technical writers. They may need to develop new standard operating procedures (SOPs). These are step-by-step instructions for how to do a job. SOPs guarantee that a job is done the same way every time.

DTs also need other abilities. One is stamina. This is the strength needed to do a long, hard job. DTs often work long hours. They may have to move and use heavy equipment. Their job also requires a lot of thought. This requires mental stamina.

A data center technician must also have a calm presence. This job can be very stressful. Remaining calm is important when

DTs take notes to use when writing instructions about how a network is configured. This helps other DTs troubleshoot problems that may arise later on.

people are waiting for a network to be fixed. It can be even more crucial when a repair doesn't work.

TRAINING TO BE A DATA CENTER TECHNICIAN

People need to train to become a DT. They can do this in several ways. Some people earn certifications. Others may attend boot camps. People who want to become DTs can also learn on their own.

Taking classes at a college is an option as well. People might earn a 2-year degree. Others earn a 4-year degree. But getting a degree isn't needed to become a DT.

Some data centers train new DTs through apprenticeships. These are periods of time spent learning from experienced professionals in the field.

BECOMING CERTIFIED

Many people who want to become DTs earn certificates. A certificate is an official document. It says that the person is trained to do a job. Some schools offer certificates. Professional organizations offer certificates, too.

Kristina Korshunova is a DT at Google. She works in New Albany, Ohio. "I've always dreamed about working at Google, so I pursued IT certificates to gain the skills that I needed," she said.[3] *IT* is short for information technology.

To earn a certificate, people like Korshunova take classes. Then they must pass a test. Certificates take less time to earn than a degree. They also cost less money. Students can earn them online.

Many online platforms and community colleges offer certifications for DTs.

One is the Cisco Certified Network Associate (CCNA) certification. Cisco is a large tech company. People who earn certificates in IT study business computing and networking.

The CCNA certification is popular in IT and DT fields. Students working on this certificate study networking, security, and programming. They don't have to have experience working as a DT. Cisco says that

Microsoft Datacenter Academy

Microsoft is committed to teaching students to work in their data centers. They work with area schools. Employees teach classes. They also mentor students. Mentors work with students one-on-one. They help them with coursework. Mentors also guide students through the process of interviewing for jobs.

In 2025, Google had 29 data centers in 11 countries around the world.

networking experience will make earning the certificate easier. An $800 training course is recommended. But students can take the exam without the course. It costs

$300 to take the exam. Students must pass the exam to earn the certification. It is valid for 3 years.

Knowing how to properly lay cable improves airflow. This keeps machines cool and prevents equipment damage.

CompTIA stands for the Computing Technology Industry Association. This professional organization offers the CompTIA A+ certificate. Students must pass two exams to earn it. In 2025, the Core 1 certification cost $265. Students can also buy study sets. Topics covered include networking, hardware, and more. The Core 2 certification also cost $265. It covers security and how to troubleshoot software issues.

Schneider Electric offers the Data Center Certified Associate certification. It is for entry-level students. They learn about the physical parts of a data center. Students study how to lay cable. They learn about cooling and preventing fires. They study power basics and generators. In 2025,

Having hands-on experience can make it easier to get a job as a DT.

the course and exam cost $250. When someone pays for the course, they have 30 days to take the exam.

BOOT CAMPS

People also attend boot camps to learn to become DTs. A boot camp is a brief, intense program. Per Scholas offers an IT Data Center Technician boot camp.

This program takes 4 months to complete. Students learn about network hardware. They study tech management. And they study security procedures.

Boot camps are like earning a certificate. The classes are usually in person. If the courses are online, they are offered in real time.

HANDS-ON EXPERIENCE

Getting a job as a data center technician can be difficult. Many people apply for each job opening. One way to have an edge is to have hands-on training.

Not all training programs provide hands-on training. Some people get it by working as an intern. Kordell Williams is a data center engineering operations technician. He works for Amazon Web Services (AWS). "I started off with an internship, which was 90 days. . . . I actually had no previous technical experience besides being able to work on a computer," said Williams.[4]

An internship is a temporary job. It is designed to help people learn about a career. Williams got a lot of hands-on experience in his internship.

Other people get hands-on experience by working related jobs. One is working as a help desk technician. Some help desk technicians work at computer stores. They help customers who buy computers. If someone has an issue with the computer, they contact the help desk. The technician asks questions about the problem.

Working as a technical support specialist is one way to gain valuable experience in fixing issues with computer hardware and software.

Sometimes they examine the computer. They may make the repair. Or they may talk the customer through the repair process.

Another way to get hands-on experience is to work as a technical support specialist. Tech support specialists work for a company. They keep the company's computer system working. Other people in this job help customers. They answer questions and troubleshoot problems. This is similar to the job of a help desk technician.

Community colleges often offer classes for those interested in pursuing a career in data center technology.

CHAPTER THREE

WORKING AS A DATA CENTER TECHNICIAN

Every day, DTs troubleshoot different issues. At least one DT is always on-site. DTs work in shifts. One person works during the day and another at night. For big jobs, several DTs work at the same time. At other times, only one DT will be on-site.

DTs working different shifts must communicate. They keep records of repairs and updates. When a DT starts their workday, they check this list. They see what

DTs must keep up with advances in new technology and have good problem-solving skills.

has been done. They look for jobs that have not been finished. DTs work together to complete tasks.

MACHINE AND NETWORK TEAMS

Companies divide their DTs into teams. Each team tackles a different set of tasks. This plan can change, such as in the event of an outage. This is when a center loses electric power. Or it's when equipment stops working. Outages can be stressful for DTs.

At Google, machine teams deal with the servers. Each of these teams is divided into two more teams. One is the project team. The other is the maintenance team. The project team updates the servers. These DTs install new equipment. They also

The Google data center in Eemshaven, Netherlands, has been fully powered by wind energy since opening in 2016. This has made power outages less of a threat.

add new servers. Then the maintenance team takes over. They fix any problems. If a server stops working, the maintenance team finds out why. The DTs on that team will make the repair.

There is a network team, too. They make sure the network is working correctly. This includes checking servers. They also check cables, switches, and routers.

Brittany Gates works at Google. She is on the network team. She must meet deadlines. It is her job to make sure things get updated on time. This means keeping up with emails and chat messages. Some days she goes to meetings. Other days she has training to learn new things.

Gates spends time every day among the servers, or on the floor. This is where she does her work. "Usually, it is 5 to 6 hours on the floor. . . . Sometimes I've had to come and work overtime because we were behind on a project," said Gates.[5]

What They Earn

The salary for data center technicians ranges from $28,000 to $74,000 per year. It varies based on education. The amount of work experience affects pay, too. What DTs earn also depends on where in the country they live. For example, those in California earn more than those in Indiana.

BEYOND THE DATA CENTER

With more experience, a DT can get a **promotion**. Some of these jobs pay more. This is because the person has more tasks to do. To receive a promotion, the employee must learn new skills.

It may take up to 2 years to get a promotion. But there are ways to speed up the process. Earning certificates such as CompTIA Network+ is a good way to learn skills. Employees also learn skills by going to college. Google pays for its employees to take college classes.

With training, a DT may become a lead DT. This person sets a maintenance schedule. They manage a team. It is their job to meet deadlines. This person has to be a good leader.

Above the lead DT is the foreman. This person is in charge of several teams. They oversee daily tasks. They work with other departments or teams. They must be a strong leader. They should be good at planning as well.

Others may be promoted to data center project manager or project engineer. They plan special projects. These might be maintenance or expansion projects. Project managers figure out project costs. They also set a schedule. Managers must know the laws or safety regulations for the projects.

Data center project managers must be good problem solvers as well. They need to be able to think ahead. If anything goes wrong, they must have a plan in place.

People who are comfortable working with computers and are well organized might be a good fit for a career as a DT.

Many managers have a college degree. A computer science degree is common. Others may have information technology degrees. Degrees in computer systems networking and telecommunications are options, too.

CHAPTER FOUR

LOOKING AHEAD

The United States Census Bureau is a federal agency. It reports on jobs in data centers. From 2016 to 2023, data center jobs grew by 60 percent. Jobs in this industry are expected to continue to grow.

People are using technology more than ever. To meet this demand, more data centers are being built each year. Many of them are bigger than existing data centers. The biggest are called hyperscale

In 2025, the largest hyperscale data center in the world was the China Telecom Data Center in Inner Mongolia.

data centers. A hyperscale data center has more than 5,000 servers. Amazon, Google, and Microsoft all have hyperscale data centers.

There is also a shortage of qualified workers. The Uptime Institute specializes in data infrastructure. In 2025, it reported that around the world 325,000 new positions needed to be filled in the data industry. This demand happened at a tough time. Many DTs were retiring. Workers were also leaving for other tech jobs. This means there were not enough qualified people to fill the jobs.

ARTIFICIAL INTELLIGENCE

Much of the growth in data centers is fueled by artificial intelligence (AI). AI is the ability of a computer to do tasks

While Microsoft has the most data centers in the world with 300, Amazon has the most hyperscale facilities.

usually done by humans. AI gathers large amounts of data. It studies the data to make connections. People are using AI to complete more tasks every day. The amount of data AI gathers is growing. Data centers store this data. Data centers must adapt. They must be more efficient. To do this, data centers have turned to AI.

AI can help predict when maintenance will be needed at data centers, which saves money and prevents outages.

AI can help with some DT tasks. Steve Santamaria leads Folio Photonics. It works to improve storage in data centers. He says:

> *AI can automate repetitive and mundane tasks, such as server monitoring . . . reducing the workload on human operators and allowing them to focus on more strategic and complex aspects of data center management.*[6]

AI can help in other ways, too. Data centers use a lot of electricity. AI can tell techs when an area needs more power. Having this information can cut down on power use. Using less power cuts costs. AI can also alert DTs when servers are overheating.

Some DTs become AI technicians. They make sure AI systems are working correctly. The AI will let DTs know which updates and

Powering AI

A ChatGPT search uses AI. It runs on computers that are in data centers. It takes ten times more electricity than a standard Google search. This increases the amount of electricity data centers need. Big tech companies are turning to nuclear power to run AI. They are also turning to wind and solar power.

repairs are needed. DTs do these repairs. As the use of AI increases, DTs will no longer monitor the network for problems. DTs will need to learn how to work with AI.

EDGE DATA CENTERS

A new kind of data center is being built. They are called edge data centers. These centers are small. They help reduce latency, or delays. This is how long it takes data to load after a request is made.

Companies that use edge data centers need to send and receive data quickly. They include cell service companies. Health care networks use edge centers, too. So do connected cars. These are cars with internet access.

In 2025, a record 4,750 data centers were under construction in the United States. This was up from about 2,000 built in 2022.

Edge data centers need DTs on staff. The teams may be smaller than at hyperscale data centers. But they still do everything to run the data center. Teams make repairs. They deal with security issues. They also handle outages. Qualified DTs will be needed to run these centers.

KEEPING CENTERS COOL

Servers create a lot of heat. Fan systems are used to keep servers cool. But using fans for cooling uses a lot of energy. It is expensive. Liquid cooling is cheaper than air cooling.

Jason Zeiler is a liquid cooling project manager at Hewlett Packard Enterprise. Zeiler explained that the newest **computer chips** don't work when they get too hot. Data center cooling is more important than ever before. "Liquid cooling for the most part is [going to] use substantially less power at the rack," said Zeiler.[7]

Liquid cooling usually uses water. It runs through pipes or tubes. The water absorbs heat from the computer. Then the water carries away the heat. DTs must understand the science of energy and heat. This helps them keep these systems running well.

DTs have an important job. But their job is changing. In the future, DTs will need to adapt. They will need to keep learning new technology. Well-trained DTs are needed to manage vast amounts of data.

Liquid cooling systems can reduce the amount of power used in a data center by 10 percent. DTs need to know how to maintain these systems.

GLOSSARY

computer chips

sets of electronic circuits on small pieces of silicon that process data in computers

diagnostic

used to identify a problem

infrastructure

the set of separate parts that makes up a network

inventory

a list of the equipment and materials on hand

optimization

making something work as efficiently as possible

promotion

a move to a job at a higher level, usually for better pay

troubleshoot

to try different ways to solve a problem

unauthorized

without permission

vendor

a person or company that sells a product or service

SOURCE NOTES

CHAPTER ONE: EXPLORING DATA CENTER TECHNOLOGY

1. Quoted in "What Is a Data Center?" *YouTube*, uploaded by Internet-Class, October 7, 2016. www.youtube.com.

2. Quoted in "How to Become a Data Center Technician? Top 5 Skills Needed to Work in a Data Center," *YouTube*, uploaded by TechTual Chatter, January 14, 2022. www.youtube.com.

CHAPTER TWO: TRAINING TO BE A DATA CENTER TECHNICIAN

3. Quoted in "A Day in the Life at Google," *YouTube*, uploaded by Google Cloud, April 3, 2024. www.youtube.com.

4. Quoted in "Working in an AWS Data Center: Meet Kordell, Engineering Operations Technician," *YouTube*, uploaded by Amazon Web Services, May 31, 2022. www.youtube.com.

CHAPTER THREE: WORKING AS A DATA CENTER TECHNICIAN

5. Quoted in "My Daily Tasks as a Data Center Technician at Google," *YouTube*, uploaded by Brittany Gates, April 20, 2025. www.youtube.com.

CHAPTER FOUR: LOOKING AHEAD

6. Quoted in Drew Robb, "AI Will Eliminate Jobs in the Data Center—But It Will Also Create New Ones," *Data Center Knowledge*, October 3, 2023. www.datacenterknowledge.com.

7. Quoted in "The Future of Liquid Cooling for Data Centers," *YouTube*, uploaded by HPE, June 20, 2024. www.youtube.com.

FOR FURTHER RESEARCH

BOOKS

Cynthia Kennedy Henzel, *Be a Cybersecurity Specialist.* BrightPoint Press, 2025.

Pamela McCauley, *Engineering for Teens: A Beginners Book for Aspiring Engineers*. Callisto Teens, 2021.

Isabel Teitelbaum, *Be a Computer Support Specialist.* BrightPoint Press, 2025.

INTERNET SOURCES

"Data Center Career Path: Fast Guide," *TechTarget*, January 4, 2020. www.techtarget.com.

"What Is a Data Center?" *Cisco*, 2025. www.cisco.com.

"What Is a Data Center Technician? 2025 Career Guide," *Coursera*, April 10, 2025. www.coursera.org.

WEBSITES

Data Center Knowledge

www.datacenterknowledge.com

Data Center Knowledge provides daily news about the data center industry. Topics include infrastructure, security, sustainability, and what to expect in the future.

Data Centre Magazine

https://datacentremagazine.com

Data Centre Magazine is a primary source of information for industry leaders. This site covers the latest news and trends.

Microsoft Datacenters

https://datacenters.microsoft.com

Microsoft Datacenters offers a variety of information on data centers. Visitors can take a virtual tour of an operating data center.

INDEX

IMAGE CREDITS

Cover: © Jacob Wackerhausen/iStockphoto
5: © Gorodenkoff/Shutterstock Images
7: © Kjetil Kolbjornsrud/Shutterstock Images
8: © IM Imagery/Shutterstock Images
11: © asharkyu/Shutterstock Images
13: © Make more Aerials/Shutterstock Images
14: © Gorodenkoff/Shutterstock Images
16: © DC Studio/Shutterstock Images
18 (data center, cables, service providers, router, computer): © Uniconlabs/Shutterstock Images
18 (modem): © Clint Kadera/Shutterstock Images
21: © Rawpixel.com/Shutterstock Images
23: © Maximumm/Shutterstock Images
25: © SeventyFour/Shutterstock Images
27: © DC Studio/Shutterstock Images
29: © Armmy Picca/Shutterstock Images
31: © Tada Images/Shutterstock Images
32: © alacatr/iStockphoto
34: © PeopleImages.com-Yuri A./Shutterstock Images
37: © DC Studio/Shutterstock Images
39: © Oleg Kovtun Hydrobio/Shutterstock Images
41: © Standret/Shutterstock Images
43: © Intreegue Photography/Shutterstock Images
47: © Gorodenkoff/Shutterstock Images
49: © XH4D/iStockphoto
51: © ShU Studio/Shutterstock Images
52: © DC Studio/Shutterstock Images
55: © Around the World Photos/Shutterstock Images
57: © Kirill Neiezhmakov/Shutterstock Images

ABOUT THE AUTHOR

Sue Bradford Edwards is a nonfiction author who writes about culture, history, and science. She enjoys helping young readers explore possible jobs. Her books about jobs include *Become a Construction Equipment Operator*, *Life as an Army Ranger*, *10 Ways to Use a Degree in Computer Science*, and *Professional Gaming Careers.*